The Language Of Despair

Whispers of a Withered Heart

Rachel Clark

BookLeaf Publishing

India | USA | UK

Made with ❤ on the BookLeaf Publishing Platform
www.bookleafpub.in
www.bookleafpub.com

Dedication

To Mr. Jamar, Mr. Rahim, Mr. Francis, and Ms. Megan; to nurse Jane, nurse Hannah, Doctor Hickey and nurse Shira; to Julia Churchill, Dayna Goldsmith and Dana Baker. For supporting me in my lowest moments, you saved my life. Thank you for the time and energy you spent looking after me and making sure I wasn't alone. I will remember you forever.

Preface

A few years ago, I decided that if I were going to live, I would commit to the journey of change and growth to blossom into the person I dreamed of being as a little girl. I resolved to experience everything and live an extraordinary life filled with love and adventure. After five mental health hospitalizations, multiple suicide attempts, and self-harm scars I am still here; surviving every traumatic experience that has come my way. "The Language of Despair: Whispers of a Withered Heart" expresses my innermost thoughts and emotions, capturing my journey of self-discovery and what it truly means to be alive - not just to survive. I am learning what it is to love; to love myself, express who I am, and connect with others after feeling isolated for so long. I hope you connect with my poetry and allow yourself to live an extraordinary, beautifully wild life and make your younger self proud of the person you have become. It will all be worth it in the end.

Acknowledgements

In the quiet corners of my heart, where shadows dance and whispers linger, this collection of poetry, "The Language of Despair, Whispers of a Withered Heart" has taken form. I am profoundly grateful to you, dear reader, for embarking on this journey with me. Your willingness to explore the depths of emotion and the intricacies of the human experience is a gift that inspires every word penned within these pages.

Faceless

I am the one that sheds your tears
The one that haunts you in your every dream
I crumple and destroy your reality
Burn your hopes into flames
I stomp and defeat every waking heartbeat
Of any being who stands in my perception

I'll make you scream and you cry
Make you wish you had died
I'll whisper in your ear till I drive you insane
Shouts to deafen your spirits and brain
Hopeless and helpless I'll leave you in pain
I'll test your reality turn it to a game
Creep demons and creatures into your veins

I'll make you befriend your worst enemies
Make you lash out at friends
Turning relationships into dead ends,
And once they betray you sweet child
You'll be a small lonely island amongst thousands of
miles

Hazel Eyes

Some days my eyes sparkle like shimmering glass
As it washes upon the shore
Like flecks of sunlight reflecting across the room
Like showers of stars enveloping the night sky

And when I look in the mirror
She stands tall and confident and beautifully
In a way I never could
But somehow her is me and she is her and we are us

And I am merely my own soul yet so broken
Lost in shambles by the darkness that consumed me
The center of my being has divided
Leaving a ghost in a crowded room

Darling

Cry me a river of tears, my darling,
For I have never loved you.

Whisper in my sorrowed ear
That I'll one day regret
All my burned bridges and tortured endings

So holler in fear, cry out for help
But you are alone my darling
No fairytale ending no beautiful wedding
The dreams you've poured your soul into

Every victory of anger and manipulation
Cry me those sacred tears, little angel
For one day your soul will burn in the
Heavens as a shimmering beam of light

Maybe one day you can fight
But now I control you and your might
Say goodbye to your life and the girl you thought you
knew
My precious you will be shiny and clean and sparkling
new

Your life now awaits, in bashes and flames,
Good luck on your own, you are alone.

My Heart's Desire

I come from a family
One of perceived wealth and deep misunderstanding
I've spun a tale that I adore
A life that's different from my core

I came from a place where the only traditions heed
From supposed blessings from the skies
Sacred promises and strict rules
We had to follow and keep till we fly

I want a beautiful family, a beautiful life
Full of pleasantries, travel, wealth, divine
I want a few lovely children, a partner who cares
Someone and something to call me mine

I am my own soul, created by fire
I work hard for my earnings, I'm drained and I'm tired
I have tried the life of countless deaths
Tried to count my blessings and give up what's left

But when I go to sleep at night
Dim the world, extinguish the light
Wearing a guise of sorrowed sighs
I hope I'm more than this disguise

Intimate Dependency

Everything in this world feels so dreadfully fake,
So incredibly fake but painfully real,
Stale and rehearsed, put up for show,
Masks and posts I'll never expose.

Put on a smile like everyone else,
A foolproof façade, concealing ourselves,
In fleeting moments it falls away,
The truth spills out in disarray.

My poor crippled heart,
She can't help but cry,
Emotions and feelings going sky high,
Dividing my mind with passing time.

Splitting and breaking I just can't combine,
Deception, reality, I'm lost and confined,
Alone and afraid from anyone else,
Except one soul who knows myself.

They'll piece me together, softly and still,
Remind me I'm strong and what I've fulfilled,
A journey through life, tougher than most,
You're strong little angel, you know how to cope.

Parts of my life seem so intensely real,
The nightmares and trauma all but distill,
Fear in my mind, distress in my thoughts,
With every heartbeat anxiety knots.

He'll hold me tight and calm my fears,
Give me warmth a strong embrace,
Of passion and heartache he calms my tears,
Streaming drops down my face

Tell me I'm safe, tell me I'm okay,
I'm strong and beautiful and don't need to fake,
A mask of perfection to shield my face,
Every moment of time I'm allowed to break.

The good and the bad intertwine, my child,
It shapes you, molds you, lets you run wild.
You're talented love, a soul so rare,
With wisdom beyond what you can bear.

I'll teach you to smile, to laugh with delight,
Reveal your true self, shine through the night,
I'll show you discomfort and how to feel safe,
When the world seems against you you'll learn not to
break.

I love you, little one, I'll always be near,
Supporting you gently to calm every fear,
Promise me once, every day,
You'll do your best and find your own way.

I'll give you the world my darling,
Peace, patience, love and understanding;
One day you'll be mine and I'll be yours,
Together we'll stand, facing life's shores.

Ghosts of a Lost Connection

Hold me close in your embrace,
Though your heart rejects my touch,
Gaze at me with eyes so dim,
Once sparkling with love's sweet rush.

Kiss me with your precious lips,
Crafted stone cold and unmoved-

I remember a time when I was your world,
When my smile was the sun,
My eyes were the stars,
Every golden speck reflected in the sky.

And once, my voice was the breeze,
Drifting afar ore every open sea;
Once, you were my comfort,
My home, a shelter of love and safety.

You'd kiss my lips fruitfully,
Drinking of sweet nectar.

But when tears came from my eyes,
The skies would weep, and joy would fade,

Turning wonderland to shattered dreams,
In the ruins of love we once made.

A Mortal's Desire

I dreamed a dream
That I wasn't forced by constraints
Wasn't human or real by any figure of life
A beautiful creature with a soft sweet smile
Who sang a siren's song

I dreamed a dream that I could be free
That I could listen and move with the breeze
Untouched by gravity, free from all ties
Not defined by a face, nor judged by my cries
No life or sorrow to meet my demise

Red Rose Embrace

My moonlight will shine upon a red rose
And only who sees it indisputably knows
The beauty and care the sky above took
To encircle that flower, a gem often forsook

A red petaled rose, the purest form made
Deep scarlet round flame, the center in shade
The secret it keeps, it's leaves tightly spun
Locks enemies out, not thinking to run

Those brave and selfish reach forward and snatch
Her secret hid deeply in your heart to match
So when you get the choice to steal a young flower
Don't step too close- it's thorns will shower

Mercilessly they'll rain, the innocence she owns
The pearls she clutches, secluded to bones
Hissing when you step too close and laughing when you
step too far
This little red flower always knows where you are

Raindrops

A young sweet child born of sadness and pain
Never something more precious ever cried in the rain
Barefooted and lost I wasn't the same
Exhausted, I fell in the street with no shame

I held back my head patterned with stains
Of raindrops and tears blending all down my face
I curled up small from the cold and embrace
The darkness inside me whispered your name

A snippet in time, it's only a trace
Of what I have lived through every day
Endless hiding striving to keep up the pace
Left shadows of terror, invading away

It's hard to feel safe, I wake with a shriek
Haunted by nightmares that linger and creep
Each night feels relentless, the silence feels bleak
In search of a haven, a place I can keep

Belonging to the Deep

Suspended in death, so beautiful, still,
Painlessly let my soul bend to its will,
The weight of the world pulling me tight,
Quieting screams, swallowed by night.

Simply

Sleep with the whales deep in the sea,
Stay with me through plummeting darkness,
Whispers and shadows beneath,
Give me hope, give me fear, give me peace.

Blissful peace thoughts erased,
Bubbling silence, time slows its pace,
Pressure holding my body in place,
Cradling me in this timeless space.

Drag me down slowly but never expect,
To see the surface no returning yet,
We'll keep you as long as is worthy,
Forsaken pet.

You belong to the ocean, belong to the deep,
Where blue lips whisper and pale skin sleeps,

Nibble her toes, mask her grace,
She'll be soon gone forever without a trace.

15

Let it swallow you up, make to erase,
Every shred of reality, every embrace,
Of beautiful, tragic, horrible fate,
Engulfed by the sea, too soon; too late.

Keep my memories, keep my mind,
All I feel is lost, confined,
Give me a place to cry, to mourn
Where I can fade and be reborn.

Hourglass

Empress of heartbreak and deception's guise
Cross me once you'll meet your demise
These stories I've lived I wish would erase
Blindly disappear without a trace

Let them swallow you up and leave you to rot
The memories, thoughts, emotions forgot
Release them to rest, let them drift away
Lost in echoes of a time gone astray

Lost timelessly places we cannot accept
Moments of sorrow we've endlessly wept
Holding fears to our hearts we tread
Seeking the light where our hopes have been fed

Into the world, I quietly step
Socially awkward, try to forget
I'll do what I can, I'm trying my best
Navigating life, seeking solace and rest

Simulations

I used to think I could swerve off the road and crash
Crash and burn and die
And I'd return to the road, I'd be alright
Like a video game, I'd reset the night

I could go off the road and be fine
No scratches of bruises, no tears of pain
I'd drive off the road in the rain
And nothing would happen, I'd just be the same

This world is a story, it's only a game
All the moments before this I've learned to play
To set my emotions deep down in my veins
I'll never be hurt though I'm never quite sane

Fluorescent Lights

They carved my skin along my side,
Marks of hands that toiled and tried,
Into my neck, a scar stretching wide,
A penrose, a chest tube, a drain aside

Daily doses of meds to help the pain,
Stabbing and pricking into my veins,
We need your blood for tests to run,
Just a quick draw, and then you're done

Succumbed to the lonely hospital bed,
Obey and relax and respect they said,
Once you're all better we'll let you eat,
For now just sleep, try and find your peace.

Moonlit Reflections

I sometimes relive my nightmares
I find a special kind of peace in the dark
It's something I can't describe with any name
But I am drawn to pain

For the beauty it brings,
The truth it beholds
My scars are the most beautiful part
Of my body and soul

Flickering Stars

I've heard I'm exquisite from plenty of people,
That I'm stunning and smart,
That I'm different, that I gave them a new start;
But I can't believe it in my heart.

What if my deepest fear comes true,
What if my existence emits to nothing,
Only a wisp in the wind of the universe...

Echoes of Long Ago

Long ago I would have liked to scream
Long and shrill, a bleeding daydream
Long ago I would climb trees
Catching the wind and scraping my knees
I would read books past my bedtime
Only 'till demons caught me in my dreams

Long ago I was hurt but kept going
I never let anyone see the wounds I was holding
But even then I would take everyone's pain
Crying out bleeding, nobody hears 'till it's too late

Long ago I made many memories
But I can't remember anymore
My mind's taken damage it's tryna restore
Protect me from my terrors, they are at war
Not long ago I saw some spirits and gore

Horror only for me, created in the depths of my core
Laughing ghosts taunt me always begging for more
I felt them to my core, but they weren't real
So later I cut and bled and didn't feel

Nightmares

Tug at the snag of the nail in my skin
Curiously watch me bleeding of sin
Blazing eyes set flame by the depths of hell
Was sent to feast by the devil himself

Laughing and crying and tears spilling wildly
'Or the dark looming cliff of the night
Demons and jokers, killers and clowns
Come out, come out to play

They'll cut you and bleed you, torment you
Deplete you, forever in permanent bond
They'll drug you and rape you, stab you and seize you
Leaving a doll wasted in pain

Steal my lips and grab my tongue
Brand their letters one by one
I cry into my dreams each night
Hoping one day I have the courage to fight

Shackled In Fear

I've never felt so lonely,
Laying here in this bed,
Day after endless day,
Night after tortuous night...

Restlessness cripples through my veins,
Doubt and worry cloud my brain,
Stuttering time that never does cease,
Exhaustingly begging for a moment's release.

Hours spent staring at the wall,
Glossy eyes close as salty tears fall,
In silence, I battle the weight of my fears,
Remembering the time I fell on deaf ears.

We're going to force this down your throat,
Going to feed you and not let you cope,
Horrendous screams I'm wailing my pleas,
Begging and sobbing down on my knees.

Let them hold you down, let them hurt you,
Make someone stay here to watch
Shrieking and screeching I tore at the sheets
Praying and pleading the torment to cease.

Attack me in panic, needles unhinged,
Restrained to the bed, anxiety spins,
Everything precious taken away,
Trashed and left in confinement to stay.

I'm scared and alone restraints gone red,
I've been screaming and pulling with all I have left,
Leave me to breathe, leave me to rest,
In this darkened abyss I long to feel blessed.

Mama

Cry all day and night,
Just tryna tell mama to turn on the light,
The monsters ignite, calling my name,
Only to hear me scream out in pain.

Mama where are you please open the door,
My dreams turn to nightmares more and more,
I've been sobbing for you to end my fear,
But soon enough I wiped my tears.

I faced my demons one by one,
Desperate for a life you could never have shown me,
I needed you mama and you weren't there,
For years of my life I've been lone without care.

Your disgusting thoughts gave me pain,
Which led to the blood I dripped from my veins,
I spilled it mama while crying your name,
For your boundless anger and constant blame.

Tell me a secret, they softly whisper,
I gave up a piece of my soul just to quiver,
For endless anxiety crippled my mind,
Then depression set in, after some time.

With your constant affliction, self-abuse and shame,
It brought me panic disorder and pain,
My poor lil sis is fighting it too,
At the same age I was, with a similar view.

You're trying to fix it but is it too late?
My whole life you left me to desecrate.
Now you're tryna do better but you have no trust,
From me or them or any of us.

I screamed on those sleepless nights,
Just pleading for a small kiss goodnight,
But I quickly stopped and you wanna know why?
It's 'cause no one was coming to turn on the light.

I was left in the darkness alone, afraid,
But I learned to adjust and hide it away,
I built a home for me and my future will stay,
I stopped ending my life and tried another way.

I learned how to fight the poison mama,
If only you had learned before all that trauma.

It's the Little Things

Waking up sprawled in my bed,
My sweet little kitty resting her head,
Walking outside, feeling the air
Cold and refreshing, I love it out there.

Drinking my tea, my juice, my drink,
Eating my favorite childhood treat,
Moments of quiet, of undisturbed sleep,
Without the distractive whirl of machines.

Sparkling cider on New Year's Eve,
Dressing up scary for Halloween,
Putting up the Christmas tree,
Covered in lights so it can be seen.

Waking up in the middle of the night,
To go for a long midnight drive,
Look at the stars, reflecting the light,
Of my loved ones who once were alive.

Flying a plane up in the sky,
Looking down on the world from so high,
Coming back to familiar home to unpack,
After a trip to the Amazon and back.

Putting on pointe shoes, ballet class,
Warm flowing water running down my back,
Brushing my teeth, taking a shower,
Let me smell like a ravishing flower.

Long rehearsals leading every night,
Till the theater becomes my life,
Stunning shows that ended just right,
Sweaty and breathless, worth the strife.

Getting my hair done, washing my face,
Changing my jewelry to keep up the pace,
Doing my makeup pretty one day,
Putting together cute outfits in May.

Swinging off a bar for trapeze,
Climbing a pole, metal between my knees,
Getting stronger and faster with practice,
Making progress towards my dreams.

Time with my family, hanging with friends,
Working and hustling before the day ends.

Tranquility

A moment of silence in a world of chaos
The distilled lilac lighting through the
Streaked cracked windows
As if the world outside this precious bubble cried

Weeping tears of lonely faces always
Monstrous to their image
Shimmering hues of purples and blues
She coats every beautiful cue

As if we frosted over in the deep of cold October

Hold me in the dazzling sights
Of illusion and beautiful deception
The highs over dream and reality
It brought me priceless moments of quiet